Being Abused While Teleworking During Coronavirus Disease 2019 (COVID-19) Pandemic

A Safety Guide for Victims of Domestic Abuse/Violence & Awareness for Bystanders

By

Mildred D. Muhammad

Being Abused While Teleworking During Coronavirus Disease 2019 (COVID-19) Pandemic: A Safety Guide for Victims of Domestic Abuse/Violence & Awareness for Bystanders

Copyright ©2020 by Mildred D. Muhammad

All rights reserved. No part of this publication may be reproduced, distributed, or transmitted in any form or by any means, including photocopying, recording, or other electronic or mechanical methods, without the prior written permission of the publisher.

ISBN: 979-8629805656

Nonfiction > Business & Economics > Decision-Making & Problem Solving

Nonfiction > Family & Relationships > Conflict Resolution

First Edition: March 2020

Independently Published

For more information, contact Mildred D. Muhammad at Mildred@myfocusllc.com.

As I'm writing, my heart is heavy because I know, right at this moment, someone (*women, men and children*) is being abused and traumatized. They feel alone and scared while being afraid to reach out!

80% of victims do not have physical scars to prove they are being victimized.

Up to 75% of victims that try to leave an abusive relationship are hurt or killed.

Stop asking victims, "why do they stay"? and start asking abusers, "why do they abuse"!

The abuse is **NOT** the victims' fault regardless of the circumstances!

The National Hotline for Domestic Violence

24 hours/7 days a week

800-799-SAFE (7233)

Table of Contents

Introduction

What is COVID-19 Pandemic?

Being Abuse While Teleworking

Bystanders (*Passive vs Active*)

Employers' Level of Responsibility

Safety Guidelines

Safety Plan

Resources

Introduction

Life, as we have known it, has changed because of the Coronavirus Disease 2019 (COVID-19). It has become a pandemic.

What is a pandemic? A disease that is prevalent over a country or the world. It is reported that every country is affected and must change the way they operate in order to bring this virus under control in their areas.

In the United States, teleworking was an option for employers to consider and has now become a reality. Many employers, large and small, have closed their businesses with the efforts of slowing down the spread of this virus because close contact is one way of passing the virus onto others.

This guide will address the abuses victims of domestic abuse and violence are facing during this pandemic. Also keep in mind that domestic violence is a worldwide epidemic.

Understanding the danger to the victims' safety and how to assist them is imperative. As a society, we must expand our view of how teleworking as well as government shutdowns are affecting those who are experiencing abusive and traumatic experiences during these times.

What is COVID-19 Pandemic?

According to the World Health Organization (WHO), *"Coronavirus disease (COVID-19) is an infectious disease caused by a newly discovered coronavirus. Most people infected with the COVID-19 virus will experience mild to moderate respiratory illness and recover without requiring special treatment. Older people, and those with underlying medical problems like cardiovascular disease, diabetes, chronic respiratory disease, and cancer are more likely to develop serious illness. The COVID-19 virus spreads primarily through droplets of saliva or discharge from the nose when an infected person coughs or sneezes, so it's important that you also practice respiratory etiquette (for example, by coughing into a flexed elbow). Currently, there are no specific vaccines or treatments for COVID-19. However, there are many ongoing clinical trials evaluating potential treatments.* https://www.who.int/health-topics/coronavirus#tab=tab_1

According to the Centers for Disease Control and Prevention (CDC), *"Coronavirus disease 2019 (COVID-19) is a respiratory illness that can spread from person to person. The virus that causes COVID-19 is novel coronavirus that was first identified during an investigation in Wuhan, China. The first case of COVID-19 in the United States was reported on January 21, 2020."* https://www.cdc.gov/.

Being Abused While Teleworking

As COVID-19 continues to change the way American business owners operate their businesses, the subject of teleworking began to become an option. And that day, for victims, became the scariest issue to accept. There are some government agencies as well as private companies that did not have teleworking as a part of their operations. However, each day brings different issues as the spread of the virus continues.

My initial thought was, what will victims and survivors do now? Going to work offered relief to their situation for 6 – 10 hours or longer. They had a sense of *'normalcy'* during the day to prepare themselves for what was to come in the evening. And now, they have nothing! They wake up to the uncertainty of what the abusers' behavior will be moment by moment.

Even though designated times are set up for teleworking, victims will have to determine their ability to perform the work. For example:

- ➢ Communicating with co-workers of the opposite sex will create insecurity with the abuser and the issue of infidelity will arise.
- ➢ Sabotaging work times, (*internet connection, phone services issues, unable to find the personal and work phone*) will cause the employer to notice productivity issues.

> Abusers will feel inadequate when they notice the level of responsibility the victim has and will begin to wonder why the victim has not left the relationship. This will increase the abusers' anxiety and cause more verbal abuse to ensue.
> If children are home, they will be left unattended during those times designated for work, again creating productivity issues.

Victims will always be on alert. They will be forced to create new coping mechanisms that will help them to establish a balance between work and home.

Unfortunately, sleeping will become their only escape and it won't be easy. Every morning victims open their eyes; they will strategize how to maneuver the next set of abuses for the day. The abusive behavior maybe the same and it will be different. Managing them, so the work can be accomplished, is the overall task of the day.

Now that the teleworking is a reality, another fact has come to mind…the abuse, emotionally and physically, will be ongoing and no one will come to help! Not that anyone has come before. But, at least going to work offered the opportunity to reach out if they needed to. Now that option is gone. Victims will begin to create different reasons to leave the home for a moment of relief.

The decision to reach out for help will not be an easy one to make. So much to consider especially if children are involved. They know that the circumstances **BEFORE** teleworking began are the same and it will be difficult to convince others that they need help. There are those who will use that excuse as a reason NOT to help. Most of society believe that victims choose to be in an abusive relationship especially those who have not experienced abuse.

Although family, friends and co-workers maybe aware of the abuse, because of COVID-19, victims are afraid they may have forgotten about them since everyone is taking extra precautions in taking care of their own families. And because of that, no one is calling to check on them. They are alone and scared.

The Abuser

COVID-19 is a gift to the abuser. Isolation has been the goal from the beginning. Abusers know they don't have to do or say anything anymore to control the victim. COVID-19 did the work for them. This quarantine, self-isolation has prevented the victim from going anywhere alone. They must inform the abuser of their whereabouts. The level of freedom, they once had, is no more. That's a significant adjustment to make.

Dr. Jekyll is alive, well and in the open. There is no need for Mr. Hyde (*Hide*) anymore because no one can come over to visit and the abuser doesn't have to go to work. Dr. Jekyll is allowed to grow and continue to terrorize the victim and their children without worrying about being exposed. The abuser views the isolation as a win-win situation. They are very aware that no one will come, and the victim is too afraid to reach out for help!

Bystanders (Active vs Passive)

What is a bystander? A bystander is a person who is present at an event or incident but does not get involved, according to the dictionary.

Everyone is a bystander from time to time. We make decisions to be passive or active regarding sporting event, concerts, and other activities. We also make the decision to be passive or active when we notice situations that we know are not right. Bystanders, during COVID-19, can be roommates, neighbors, children, family, at times co-workers during a conference call or video chat.

To participate or get involved in an event or help someone is an active bystander. And NOT participating or getting involved to help someone is a passive bystander. When the event/situation arrives, you will determine which one you are!

Intervening in an abusive relationship is not one to take lightly. Many people feel if they reach out to help, the victim will take the abusers' side and return to the relationship. So, what is the point in helping?

I do not advocate for anyone to put themselves in harm's way trying to help their friend, family member or colleague. And at the same time, if you know someone who is being abuse, don't look away! Just remember to call the police!

Establishing healthy boundaries for yourself as well as the victim will be the determining factor for your level of assistance. When in doubt, call the police. They are trained to handle domestic disputes.

Below are boundaries to consider establishing **BEFORE** moving forward:

- Decide what you will do, what you won't do and what you can't do!
- If you know your friend, family member or colleague is in an abusive relationship, stay in contact with them so they can have a lifeline outside the home. Setup a code text or word that will indicate you are in trouble and to call the police.
- If you have a significant other, discuss your boundaries as a unit and decide the best strategy to assist without putting yourselves in harm's way.
- If you hear your neighbor being abused, don't be afraid to contact the police.
- If there is a suspension of abuse, contact the police and request a wellness check.

Don't give up on them because they won't leave. Shelters and transitional homes are full. COVID-19 is the reality of the day and their home is all they have right now.

Be patient, non-judgmental and kind. They don't need to be victim-blamed for a situation out of their control. They need to be supported not condemned.

Employers' Level of Responsibility

Domestic abuse and violence don't have an educational, occupational or financial status. This issue **IS** within the workplace! The responses of most businesses:

- It is ignored
- The victim, not the abuser, is held accountable

Many believe the employer is not responsible for their employees' personal life, even when there is an issue brought to their attention. They feel that since they are not able to ask questions, during the interview session, about their personal lives, then situations that arise after employment is the employees' responsibility to handle without their assistance and it should not affect their productivity.

As with any personal issue that may arise, employees are aware of the stigma that will be attached to them should they decide to inform management of a problem. It is as if a target has been placed on their back because now everything that they do will be documented towards the possibility of being terminated should their productivity decreases.

In this climate of teleworking, employers must develop a system of wellness checks to ensure their employees are safe and able to reach out should an incident arise.

Below are suggested guidelines to consider:
- Employers should establish a code that alerts the employer of a case of domestic violence while working strategically with the victim to ensure their safety.
- Establish a 30-minute video call to be placed on the victims' calendar to be determined by the employee and the employer.
- Employers must insist the employee is *"live"* in a video conference call and not accept a stock photo.
- Don't assume that a logged in employee represented online is the employee. Ask questions, only the employee would know, to identify their presence.
- During the call, be aware of any odd noises that occur during an audio call and odd positions during a video.
- Insist on a daily check in when you notice issues with productivity.
- If there is a suspension of abuse, contact the police and request a wellness check. The abuser

will recognize that someone is watching and my limit the abusive behavior.

These measures, along with others, can help to ensure that victims of domestic violence have a way to communicate their abuse and the abuser will recognize that they are not as in control of the victim as they thought.

Safety Guidelines for Victims

If you are a victim and teleworking is a reality, I know you're scared and may feel alone. Here are a few suggestions to consider:

- ➢ Determine the best strategy to use in order to be safe and/or when to leave.
- ➢ Secure your work material in one location so if you need to leave abruptly, you can grab it and go!
- ➢ As you are working and you determine you need help, send a coded email, to someone you know who always checks their email to call the police. Follow up with this text message: *"Check your email"*.
- ➢ Setup a text number for family and friends. When they receive the text, with those numbers, they will know to call the police.
- ➢ Strategically, hide 3 days of clothing and all vital information (*a complete list is in the safety plan*)

in your vehicle, preferably the trunk. (*Don't do this all in one trip as suspension will rise in your abuser*).
➢ Tell the abuser you're hungry. Call 911 to order a pizza. This has occurred several times throughout the nation. Dispatchers are aware of these calls.

Don't blame yourself for your situation. The abuse is **NOT** your fault.

Comprehensive Safety Plan

The Hardest Decision

Planning to leave an abusive relationship is the hardest decision to make. So many things to take into consideration (*where will you go, legal steps, uprooting children, explaining to others, etc.*). Others may feel that your reasons for leaving are not valid. Just because you don't have physical scars doesn't mean you are not a victim or survivor. 80% of victims/survivors don't have physical scars to prove their abuse.

When you are in this type of situation, it is very important that you understand that NO ONE understands your condition better than you. They are not there with you when the abuse takes place. There isn't any way of knowing what your abuser will do next. Therefore, you are the best person to make this decision.

A safety plan is one of the best tools you can have when trying to make the best decision for yourself and your children. This safety plan is a comprehensive, step-by-step plan to assist you in eight areas of your life. All you must do is fill in the blanks. **Hide this plan so your abuser will not discover your next move.** Email it to a trusted friend or relative. As a matter of fact, only tell one person (*a trusted friend or relative*) what you intend to do. Any more than one will hamper your efforts to leave, because you don't know who your abuser knows.

And once the abuser knows, your plan is out the window.

Leaving an abusive relationship is the most dangerous time for you. Why? Because the abuser will feel that the control is no longer there. Which makes the abuser a very dangerous person and all rational is non-existent.

Leaving is also hard because you begin to remember the loving times in that relationship and of the many years you have put into it. Then the thoughts of *'how did we get here'* will surface.

Listen, YOU know your abuser better than anyone. Rely on what you know and use it to your benefit. Follow your spirit, it will not lead you astray. Pray and ask God for guidance. Ask Him to put people and resources in place to help you.

Only YOU will know when it is time to leave. Don't be so concerned with what your abuser is feeling that you stop caring about your safety. Always remember, it is NOT your fault and it is never too late to stand up for yourself. However, be wise, strategic and careful.

The 24-hour National Hotline for Domestic Violence is 800-799-SAFE (7233).

The following steps represent my plan for increasing my safety and preparing in advance for the possibility for further violence. Although I do not have control over my partner's violence, I do have a choice about how to respond to him/her and create the best strategy for myself and my children to be safe.

STEP 1: Safety during a violent incident.

Women cannot always avoid violent incidents. In order to increase safety, battered women may use a variety of strategies.

I can use some or all the following strategies:

A.   If I decide to leave, I will _____
_____*(Practice how to get out safely. What doors, windows, elevators, stairwells, or fire escapes would you use?)*

B.   I can keep my purse and car keys ready and put them *(place)* _____ in order to leave quickly.

C.   I can tell _____
about the violence and request they call the police if they hear suspicious noises coming from my house or apartment.

D.   I can teach my children how to use the telephone to contact the police and the fire department.

E.   I will use _____ as my code word with my children and my friends so they can call for help.

F.   If I must leave my home, I will go _____
_____*(Decide this even if you don't think there will be a next time.)* If I cannot go to the location above, then I can go to _____ _____ or _____ _____.

G.   I can also teach some of these strategies to some/all my children.

H.   When I expect we are going to have an argument, I will try to move to a space that is lowest risk, such as _____.
(Try to avoid arguments in the bathroom, garage, kitchens, near weapons or in rooms without access to an outside door.)

I.   I will use my judgment and intuition. If the situation is very serious, I can give my partner what he/she wants to calm him/her down. I must protect myself until I/we are out of danger.

STEP 2:   Safety when preparing to leave.

Battered women frequently leave the residence they share with their abuser. Leaving must be done with a careful plan in order to increase safety. Abusers often strike back when they believe that their victim is leaving a relationship.

I can use some or all the following safety strategies:

A.   I will leave money and an extra set of keys with _____ so I can leave quickly.

B.   I will keep copies of important documents or keys at _____.

C.   I will open a savings account by _____ _____ to increase my independence.

D.   Other things I can do to increase my independence include: _____
_____
_____
_____.

E.   The domestic violence national hotline number is (800)-799-SAFE (7233). My local coalition phone number is _____. I can seek shelter by calling both numbers.

25

F. I will check with _____ and _____ to see who would be able to let me stay with them or lend me money.

G. I can leave extra clothing with _____ _____.

H. I will sit down and review my safety plan every _____ in order to plan the safest way to leave my residence. (*Domestic violence advocate or friend*) _____has agreed to help me review this plan.

I. I will rehearse my escape plan and, as appropriate, practice it with my children.

STEP 3:   Safety in my own residence.

There are many things that a woman can do to increase her safety in her own residence. It may be impossible to do everything at once, but safety measures can be added step by step.

Safety measures I can use include:

A.   I can change the locks on my doors and windows as soon as possible.

B.   I can replace wooden doors with steel/metal doors.

C.   I can install security systems including additional locks, window bars, poles to sedge against doors, an electronic system, etc.

D.   I can purchase rope ladders to be used for escape from second floor windows.

E.   I can have smoke detectors installed and purchase fire extinguishers for each floor in my house/apartment.

F.   I can install an outside lighting system that lights up when a person is coming close to my house.

G.   I will teach my children how to use the telephone to make a call for me and to _____ _____(friend/minister/other) in the event that my partner takes the children.

STEP 4:   **Safety with a protection order**

Many batterers obey protection orders, but one can be sure which violent partner will obey and which will violate protection orders. I recognize that I may need to ask the police and the courts to enforce my protection order.

The following are some steps that I can take to help the enforcement of my protection order:

A.   I will keep my protection order _____
_____ (*location*). (*Always keep it on or near your person. If you change purses, that's the first thing that should go in.*)

B.   I will give my protection order to police departments in the community where I work, in those communities where I usually visit family or friends, and in the community where I live.

C.   There should be a county/parish registry of protection orders that all police departments can call to confirm a protection order. (NCIC) I can check to make sure that my order is in the registry. The phone number for the county registry of protection orders is _____.

D.   For further safety, if I often visit other counties/parishes, I will file my protection order with the court in those counties/parishes under Full, Faith and Credit. I will register my protection order in the following counties/parishes: _____

_____ and __
_____.

E.   I can call the local domestic violence program if I am not sure about B., C., or D. above or if I have some problem with my protection order.

F.   I will inform my employer, my minister, my closest friend, and _____
_____ that I have a protection order in effect.

G.   If my partner destroys my protection order, I can get another copy from the courthouse.

H.   If my partner violates the protection order, I can call the police and report a violation, contact my attorney, call my advocate, and/or advise the court of the violation.

I.   If the police do not help, I can contact my advocate or attorney and will file a complaint with the Chief of the police department.

J.   I can also file a private criminal complaint in the jurisdiction where the violation occurred with the District Attorney. I can charge my battering partner with a violation of the protection order and all the crimes that he commits in violating the order.

STEP 5: Safety on the job and in public.

Each battered woman must decide when she will tell others that her partner has abused her and that she may be at continued risk. Friends, family and co-workers can help to protect women. Each woman should consider carefully which people to invite to help secure her safety.

I might do any or all the following:

A.   I can inform my boss, the security supervisor and _____ at work of my situation.

B.   I can ask _____ to help screen my telephone calls to work.

C.   When leaving work, I can _____
_____
_____
_____.

D.   When driving home, if problems occur, I can
_____
_____
_____.

E.   If I use public transportation, I can _____
_____
_____.

F.   I can use different grocery stores and shopping malls for purchases. I can shop at hours that are different than those when residing with my abuser.

G.   I can use a different bank and take care of my banking online or at hours different from those I used when residing with my abuser.

H.   I can also _____
_____
_____.

STEP 6: **Safety and drug or alcohol use.**

Many people in this culture use alcohol. Many use mood-altering drugs. Much of this use is legal and some are not. The legal outcomes of using illegal drugs can be very hard on a battered woman. The consequences may hurt her relationship with her children and put her at a disadvantage in other legal action with her battering partner.

Therefore, women should carefully consider the potential cost of the use of illegal drugs. But beyond this, the use of any alcohol or other drugs can reduce a woman's awareness and ability to act quickly to protect herself from her battering partner.

Furthermore, the use of alcohol or other drugs by the batterer may give him/her and excuse to use violence. So, in the context of drug or alcohol use, a woman will need to make specific safety plans.

If drug or alcohol use has occurred in my relationship with the battering partner, I can enhance my safety by some or all the following:

A. If I am going to use, I can do so in a safe place and with people who understand the risk of violence and are committed to my safety.

B. I can also _____
_____
_____.

C. If my partner is using, I can _____
_____
_____.

D. I might also _____
_____
_____.

E. To safeguard my children, I will _____
_____
_____
_____
_____
_____.

STEP 7: Safety and my emotional health

The experience of being battered and verbally degraded by partners is usually exhausting and emotionally draining. The process of building a new life for myself takes much courage and incredible energy.

To conserve my emotional energy, resources AND avoid hard emotional times, I can do some of the following:

A.   If I feel down and ready to return to a potentially abusive situation, I can _____
_____
_____.

B.   When I must communicate with my abuser in person or by telephone, I can _____
_____
_____
_____.

C.   I can tell myself " _____
_____
_____

_____"whenever I feel others are trying to control or abuse me.

D.   I can call _____
_____ and _____
to help me feel stronger.

E. Other things I can do to help me feel stronger are _____, _____

and _____.

F. I can attend workshops online and join online support groups to gain confidence and strengthen my relationships with other people.

STEP 8:   Items to take when leaving

When victims leave abusers, it is important that they take certain items with them. Beyond this, women sometimes give an extra copy of papers and an extra set of clothing to a friend just in case they must leave quickly.

Items with a check mark listed below are the most important to take with you.

These items might best be placed in one location, so that if we must leave in a hurry, I can grab them quickly.

When I leave, I should take:

- ✓ Identification, Passports for myself & my children
- ✓ Birth certificates (for myself & my children}
- ✓ Social security cards
- ✓ School & vaccination records
- ✓ Money, credit cards, checkbook & ATM cards
- ✓ Keys – house/car/office
- ✓ Driver's license, insurance card & registration
- ✓ Work Permit
- ✓ Green cards
- ✓ Medications
- ✓ Medical records
- ✓ Insurance papers

Resources

National Domestic Violence 24-hour Hotline
https://www.thehotline.org/help/
800-799-SAFE (7233)

National Resource Center on Domestic Violence
https://www.nrcdv.org/
800-537-2238

National Center for Victims of Crime
https://victimsofcrime.org/
202-467-8700

National Coalition Against Domestic Violence
https://ncadv.org/get-help

Domestic Violence Coalitions are available in every state

Domestic Shelters
https://www.domesticshelters.org/

RAINN (Rape, Abuse & Incest National Network)
https://www.rainn.org/
800-656-HOPE (4673)

Domestic Violence Resources for Male Survivors
https://www.huffpost.com/entry/domestic-violence-resourc_b_10281088

About the Author

Mildred D. Muhammad is an Award-Winning Global Keynote Speaker, International Expert Speaker for the  US Dept of State, Certified Consultant with the US Dept of Justice/Office for Victims of Crime, CNN Contributor, Domestic Abuse Survivor, Certified Domestic Violence Advocate, Advisory Board Member for The National Resource Center on Domestic Violence, Sexual Assault Advocacy Network's Advisor, 5X-Author, Former Internet TV Talk Show Host, Trainer & Educator traveling and speaking on a national and international platform to discuss her life of terror, abuse and heartache, all while promoting Domestic Violence Awareness and Prevention.

As the ex-wife of the D.C. Sniper, John A. Muhammad, Mildred shares the very personal details of her experiences involving fear, abuse and many times, victim-blaming. This experience has allowed Mildred's mission to be even more influential and of a greater purpose. Simply stated, she was a victim who became a survivor and is now a warrior on the issues of domestic abuse/violence. She shares her expertise on what it's like to be a victim and a survivor of domestic violence "without physical scars" to various conferences, seminars, workshop audiences which include victims and survivors of domestic violence, advocates, law enforcement professionals, therapists, counselors, mental and medical health providers, university and college students as well as conduct military personnel training regarding domestic violence. Her authenticity is as remarkable as her unforgettable story of abuse. She explains the perils of PTSD (post-traumatic stress disorder) soldiers suffer when returning from a war zone as well as victims who are diagnosed with PTSD. She is recognized and received awards, throughout military communities, for championship of the Family Advocacy Program and their mission to educate, promote and end Domestic Violence in Military Communities.

After counseling herself and her children to survive victim-blaming through the midst of adversity, she transformed her tragic circumstances into an opportunity to establish ground on all forms of Domestic Violence that are often overlooked such as verbal, mental, economic, spiritual, stalking and emotional abuse. She not only speaks of the details and the realities of Domestic Abuse/Violence, Mildred makes it her mission to be a vessel of support and healing to all those affected.

Her first critically acclaimed memoir, Scared Silent: When the One You Love Becomes the One You Fear, was published by Simon & Schuster in 2009. Muhammad has self-published two working journals, "A

Survivor's Journal" & "Dare to Heal", as well as "Planning My Escape" (*a comprehensive step by-step safety plan*) specifically for victims and survivors to help with the emotions that others may not understand and strategically leaving an abusive relationship. Her second and last memoir, "I'm Still Standing" has been released.

She has received many awards such a Special Commendation presented by the Office on Violence Against Women, Maya Angelou "Still I Rise" Award, Shirley Chisholm Woman of Courage Award and REDBOOK's Strength & Spirit HEROES Award, as well as multiple awards from the military community...just to name a few.

Mildred Muhammad has appeared in the following TV shows: Lifetime Movie Network Series, *"Monster in My Family"*; CNN documentary, *"The Minds of the Sniper"*; TruTV documentary *"The DC Sniper's Wife"* produced by award-winning producer, Barbara Kopple; Discovery Channel, *"Who The Bleep Did I Marry"*; Investigation Channel Series, *"Escaped ~ The Sniper's Wife: Episode 2;* MSNBC documentary, *"I Married The Beltway Sniper"* and the syndicated TV show, Crime Watch Daily.

Mildred Muhammad has been interviewed on Dr. Oz, Oprah: Where Are They Now, Anderson, Ricki Lake, Katic Couric, Issues with Jane Velez Mitchell, The Mike Huckabee Show, TruTV's In Session, Larry King Live, The Tyra Banks Show, and Good Morning America, and has appeared on BET and other local and national TV interviews. She has also been interviewed by various national and international radio shows, internet radio, various national and international newspapers, and internet blogs and magazines worldwide, including the BBC, NPR, Essence, Jet, The Washington Post, and Newsweek. She has also been recognized as "One of the Nation's most powerful advocates for victims and survivors of domestic violence". WROC-TV, Rochester, NY.

For more information or to book Mildred Muhammad
for your event, visit her website,
www.MildredMuhammad.com.

Follow Mildred:

https://bit.ly/2UxzbW6

Listen to "Rising Above It All"
with Mildred Muhammad on
☐ https://anchor.fm/mildred-d-muhammad

https://bit.ly/33FcHXi

https://bit.ly/39eo49U

www.ingramcontent.com/pod-product-compliance
Lightning Source LLC
Chambersburg PA
CBHW050305220526
45465CB00002B/825